MERCY, JUSTICE AND PEACE

Selected Quotations From the
QUR'AN

Riaz Ahmad Malik

ILM PUBLICATIONS
Houston, Texas, USA
2005

© 2005 Riaz A. Malik

ISBN: 0-9769658-0-1

Library of Congress Control Number: 2005904376

Publisher:

ILM PUBLICATIONS
9720 Beechnut St. #280
Houston, Texas 77036
USA
Email: ilmrm@yahoo.com

Website: www.interfaithlearning.com

ILM is a charitable non-profit organization, established in the State of Texas, USA, under Chapter 501 (C) (3) of the Internal Revenue Code. It is dedicated to the promotion of tolerance, understanding, harmony and close cooperation among peoples of different faiths to fight the evils of bigotry, fanaticism, intolerance and ignorance. Profits from its publications and other activities are to be used in the furtherance of these goals.

CONTACT INFORMATION

Riaz A. Malik
Phone: 832 646 4646

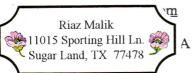

Mercy, Justice and Peace

**GOD IS THE LIGHT
OF THE HEAVENS AND THE EARTH.**

CONTENTS

Introduction
6

Fatiha (The Opening)
10

The Creator
12

The Creation
17

The Messenger
22

Mankind
27

Religious Freedom and Tolerance
30

Jews and Christians
45

Jesus
54

Social Interaction with Non-Muslims
58

All deeds have consequences
60

Only defensive war permitted
62

Piety
64

Charity
65

Justice and Fair Dealing
67

Parents
71

Miscellaneous
72

Appendix: English Translations of the Qur'an.
79

INTRODUCTION

The Qur'an, the Holy Scripture of Islam in Arabic, is a compilation of Divine Revelations (*Wahy*) received by Prophet Muhammad[s] in short segments at random intervals over a period of about 23 years of his mission from year 610 to 632 AD. These revelations were organized, on his instruction, into 114 chapters with loose subject arrangement. Soon after the death of the Prophet[s] in 632, Abu Bakr, the first Caliph, ordered the preparation of an official manuscript of the Qur'an and appointed a committee for this purpose. Collecting and verifying all of the segments memorized by the Companions of the Prophet[s] and written on miscellaneous materials, the comprehensive one-volume manuscript of the Qur'an was prepared within two years after the death of the Prophet[s]. Fifteen years later, on the orders of the third Caliph Uthman, a number of authenticated copies of this original master manuscript were prepared and placed in the depository libraries in Medina, Mecca, Damascus, Kufa (Iraq) and garrison settlements in Egypt and Iran.

In addition to the unbroken chain of the written word from the time of the Prophet[s], the memorization of a part or whole text of the Qur'an has always been considered a highly meritorious deed, and throughout the centuries, a large number of *huffaz* or reciters have committed the entire Arabic text of the Qur'an to memory. Based on these factors, the current text of the Qur'an is believed to be the same as revealed.

The Qur'an is arranged into 114 *surahs* or chapters of unequal length, the longest *surah* containing 286 verses and the shortest fitting on one line with only 10 words in three verses. In general, the arrangement of the *surahs* is based on the size, the larger chapters being placed at the beginning and smaller ones at the end. The Qur'an contains some 6236 verses, with the whole text covering about 350-400 pages of medium size.

Being a collection of short segments received over a long period of time, delivered as spoken word, and later put together into chapters, the style and arrangement of the text of the Qur'an are unique and cannot be compared to any other book. The text has a rhythmic flow, one concept submerging like a wave and giving way to another subject without any perceptible break. The text of the Qur'an, according to Muslim belief, is the word of God addressed to Prophet Muhammad[s] as the direct recipient of the revelation. Its melodic recitation has become a highly developed art, and the reciters are honored as accomplished artists in the Muslim communities.

The Qur'an is the basis of all fundamental teachings of Islam and is recognized by all Muslim sects as the final authority on all religious matters. It is revered by a billion-plus Muslims as the Holy Word of God, and memorized and recited by Arabs and non-Arabs alike in its original Arabic text.

The most essential elements of its teachings are:

- Absolute and Indivisible Unity of God,
- Unity and Equality of all Mankind,
- Unity of the Source and the Message of all the Prophets and Messengers of God, and, as a logical result,
- Basic Unity of all Religions.

According to the Qur'an, all different nations and peoples of the world have been recipients of the Divine revelation, inspiration and guidance through Messengers and Prophets (Qur'an, 35:24).

The main objective of the teachings of the Qur'an is to provide guidance for a purposeful and righteous life by developing a close and loving spiritual relationship with God and serving humanity to the best of one's abilities. The most fundamental concepts that run forcefully throughout the Quran are:

- Duties towards God and towards Humanity.
- The Importance of Righteous and Good Deeds.
- Complete Freedom of Religion.
- Peaceful co-existence with people of different faiths.
- Justice for all regardless of their Beliefs, Nationality and Social or Economic status.
- Service to Humanity through good and charitable deeds, etc.

In this monograph, a selection of the verses of the Qur'an is provided to present the fundamental Islamic teachings, with special attention to the above-mentioned concepts. Most of the selected quotations belong to the class of verses that in the Qur'an itself are referred to as *"Clear and Decisive in meaning (muhkam); they are the essence of the book."* (Qur'an, 3:7). Their authority and status are recognized as superior to any other source of the religion of Islam, and they are not subject to any interpretation that would modify or change their meanings.

The purpose of this selection is to offer some brief glimpses of the *Weltanschauung* (world-view) of the Qur'an, and to draw attention of Muslims and non-Muslims alike to the authentic beliefs of Islam. It is hoped that these quotations will help dispel the highly erroneous views about teachings of Islam on tolerance, religious freedom and peaceful co-existence, and make it evident that some of the actions carried out in the name of Islam are strictly forbidden by that religion of peace, and are indeed flagrant violations of the injunctions of the Qur'an.

In this selection, the translation of the Arabic verses into English is generally based on that of Abdullah Yusuf-Ali's original translation of the Qur'an, with changes in wording to conform to the modern English language. In addition, many translations and commentaries on the Qur'an were consulted and every effort made to present clearly the closest meanings of the verses.

It is a customary practice among Muslims to invoke the blessings of God when the name of Prophet Muhammad[s] or any of the other Prophets or Messengers of God, for example Noah[s], Abraham[s], Isaac[s], Jacob[s], Moses[s] or Jesus[s] is mentioned. In honor of that tradition, a superscript [s] has been inserted after the names of the Prophets as an abbreviation for the invocation in Arabic meaning *Peace Be Upon Him*. This insertion is not permitted in the text of the Qur'an, and where the name occurs in a verse, no superscript has been added.

Following the long-established tradition and recognized meaning by linguistic scholars, in this work the Arabic word 'Allah' has been translated as 'God.' In Arabic, the word Allah, - considered by numerous philologists to be a contraction of the words *Al* (the) and *Ilah* (God) - has been used, at least since the time of Jesus[s], by Jews, Christians, Muslims and other religious groups, as the universal name for God, and many eminent scholars and translators of the Qur'an have translated Allah into English as God. This has been done to clarify and stress the fact that Allah in Arabic and God in English are One and the Same and these terms are inter-changeable.

FATIHA
(THE OPENING)

Surah Fatiha is the opening chapter of the Qur'an and has been described as the essence of the Qur'an. These seven short verses contain, in a condensed form:

> 1. Statement of faith in God, the One and Only Lord of the Universe, Who is the Most Compassionate and the Most Merciful. (In the Muslim creed, Compassion and Mercy are the most prominent Divine attributes. The Formula *"In the name of God, Most Compassionate, Most Merciful"* is repeated dozens of times a day by observant Muslims, the purpose being to create an awareness and a desire to inculcate in themselves the Divine qualities of Compassion and Mercy).

> 2. Affirmation of human relationship with God, of exclusive worship and complete dependence.

> 3. Prayer and supplication for His Guidance and Help in finding the straight path and leading a righteous and successful life, blessed with His acceptance and pleasure.

This *surah* is memorized by almost all Muslims in the original Arabic. It is recited numerous times in all daily ritual and congregational prayers and on many other occasions and forms an essential part of a Muslim's daily life.

**IN THE NAME OF GOD
MOST COMPASSIONATE, MOST MERCIFUL**

All praise is to God
The Creator and Sustainer of the Worlds:
Most Compassionate, Most Merciful;
Master of the Day of Judgment.
You Alone we Worship,
And You only we ask for help.
Guide us in the Right Path,
The way of those whom
You have favored with Your Grace,
Not of those who have
Earned Your displeasure
Nor of those who are astray.

Qur'an, 1:1-7

THE CREATOR

الله نور
السموات
والارض

God is the Light
Of the heavens and the earth.

(Qur'an, 24:35)

Allah! There is no god But He,
- The Living, Eternal and Ever-lasting,
Supporter of all.
No slumber can overcome Him
Nor sleep. His are all things
In the heavens and on earth.

His Throne of Power extends
Over the Heavens
And the earth, and the care and
Preservation of them tires Him not.

Qur'an, 2:255

God is He, than Whom
There is no other god.
The Sovereign, the Holy One
The Source of Peace and Perfection
The Guardian, the Preserver of safety,
The Exalted in Might,
The Irresistible, the Supreme,
Glory to God:
High is He, above having
Any partners they attribute to Him.
He is God, The Creator,
The Originator, The Fashioner,
To Him belong
The Most Beautiful Names:
Whatever is in
The heavens and the earth
Declares His Praises and Glory:
And He is the
Exalted in Might, the Wise.

Qur'an, 59:23-24

Say: He is God
The One God, Eternal, Absolute,
He begets not, nor is He begotten,
And there is none
Like unto Him.

Qur'an, 112:1-4

And if all the trees
Of earth were pens
And the ocean were ink
With seven oceans behind it
To add to its supply
Yet would not the Words
Of God be exhausted
For God is Exalted, Source of Wisdom.

Qur'an, 31:27

He to Whom belongs the Kingdom
Of the heavens and the earth.
No son has He begotten,
Nor has He
Any partner in His dominion.
It is He Who created all things,
And ordered them in due proportions.

Qur'an, 25:2

Whatever is in the
Heavens and on earth
Declares the Praises and Glory
Of God, for He is the
Exalted in Might, the Wise.
To Him belongs the Kingdom
Of the heavens and the earth.
It is He Who gives Life and Death,
And He has Power over all things.
He is the First and the Last
And the Evident and the Hidden:
And He has complete knowledge
Of all things.

Qur'an, 57:1-3

See you not that it is
God whose praises all things
In heaven and on earth
Do celebrate, and the birds
In the air with wings outstretched?
Each one knows its own
Mode of prayer and praise.
And God knows well all
That they do.

Qur'an, 24:41

The seven heavens and the earth,
And all things therein,
Declare His glory:
There is nothing that does not
Celebrates His praise;
But you do not comprehend
How they declare His glory.

Qur'an, 17:44

See you not that
To God submit in worship all things
That are in the heavens and on earth,
The sun, the moon, the stars,
The hills, the trees, the animals,
And a great number among mankind?

Qur'an, 22:18

THE CREATION

Do not the Unbelievers see
That the heavens and the earth
Were one compact mass
Before
We split them apart?
We made everything living
From water.
Will they not then believe?

Qur'an, 21:30

It is He Who created
The Night and the Day.
And the sun and the moon
All float along swiftly,
Each in its own
Celestial orbit.

Qur'an, 21:33

It is God Who has created
The heavens and the earth
And He sends down rain
From the skies, thereby
Producing fruit as food for you:
It is He
Who has made the ships of service
To you, that they may sail
Upon the sea by His Command;
And the rivers also
Has He made for service to you.
And He has subjected the sun
And the moon for your benefit,
Both diligently pursuing their courses;
And the night and the day
He subjected for your comfort.
And He gives you all
That you ask for.
And if you think of the favors
Of your Lord, never will you
Be able to count them,
But surely man is
Unjust and thankless.

Qur'an, 14:32-34

Behold! In the creation
Of the heavens and the earth;
In the rotation
Of the Night and the Day;
In the sailing of the ships
Through the oceans
For the benefit of mankind;
In the rains which God
Sends down from the skies,
And the life that He gives with it
To an earth that is dead;
In the creatures of all kinds
That He has scattered through the earth,
In the change of the winds,
And the clouds which they
Trail, held in control
Between the sky and the earth:-
(In all these) Indeed are Signs
For people who use their wisdom.

Qur'an, 2:164

See you not that
God sends down rain
From the sky? With it
We then bring out produce
Of various colors.
And in the mountains
Are tracts white and red,
Of various shades of color,
And black intense in hue.
And so amongst men
And beasts and cattle
Are they of various colors.
Truly in awe of God
Among His servants
Are the scholars.
God is Exalted in Might,
Very Forgiving.

Qur'an, 35:27-28

Surely in the heavens
And the earth are Signs
For those who believe.
And in the creation of yourselves,
And in the animals He has scattered
(Through the earth), are Signs
For those who are sure in knowledge.
And in the alternation
Of Night and Day,
And in the fact that God
Sends down Sustenance
From the sky, and revives with it
The earth after its death,
And in the change of the winds-
Are signs for the people
Who use their talents.

Qur'an, 45:2-5

THE MESSENGER

Abul Qasim Muhammad *ibn Abdullah ibn Abdul Muttalib ibn Hashim, (Sall Allah-o Alaihi wa Sallam),* a descendent of Ibrahim[s] (Abraham) through his older son Ismail[s], was born in Mecca in the year 569 in Hashim clan of Quraysh tribe. Being an underprivileged orphan, he grew up to be a very sensitive and contemplative young man. He was hired by Khadija, a distant cousin and a very wealthy lady of Mecca, as a manager for her trading business. She was so impressed by his sincerity and honesty that she offered to marry him. Khadija at that time was in her thirties and Muhammad[s] was 25. Their personal life was very comfortable, but they both shared a yearning for the spiritual truth and compassion for the less fortunate, and were troubled by the evil ways of the Meccan aristocracy and their idolatry, superstitions and oppression of slaves, women, orphans and the poor in general.

Muhammad[s] was given to contemplation and serious thought from his childhood. He adopted, at the age of 35, the practice of retiring to a cave near Mecca for long retreats, spending weeks on end there in fasting, contemplating and praying for divine guidance. It was during one of these retreats that he received his first Divine revelation at the age of forty in 610. Initially, he talked about this experience to his family and friends only. The revelations continued and three years later, the public declaration of his mission and the invitation to his fellow citizens to worship God alone and to mend their vile ways was met with rejection that soon turned to vicious persecution of all who joined him. Things went from bad to worse and his whole clan was subjected to an economic and social boycott from the city, resulting in their exile to a desolate ravine outside Mecca to protect their lives. The hardships of extreme climate, starvation and thirst suffered during three long years in the bleak desert - where the days burn and the nights freeze - wreaked havoc on the health of all the clan. His loving wife Khadija, who had grown up in the lap of luxury and comfort, deprived herself of the food and drink to provide for the children. She was very weak and sick when the boycott was lifted and died soon after returning to Mecca. His aging uncle Abu Talib, the head of the clan of Hashim, who had stood by him and protected him, also succumbed to the ravages of hardships endured during these years. The new head of the clan was his sworn enemy. He withdrew the protection of the clan that was essential for any individual's survival. The conditions looked dismal, but Prophet Muhammad[s] never lost hope and continued his mission risking his life every day.

Soon a flicker of light shone from the north. The people of the city of Yathrib (later known as Medina or the City of the Prophet) invited Muhammad[s] with his followers to move to their city and accepted him as their leader. This migration or Hijra in 622 marks the start of the Islamic calendar. During the next few years, three major attacks on Medina by the Meccans were repulsed and, in less than 8 years, the exiled Prophet[s] entered as a peaceful conqueror the city he had left as a fugitive. The Meccans were treated magnanimously. By the end of his life some thirty months later almost the whole of Arabian Peninsula had accepted him as their religious and political leader.

Prophet Muhammad[s] encountered extremely difficult circumstances and overcame odds that looked insurmountable, and at the time of his death at the age of 63 in June 632, he had not only founded one of the great religions of the world, but also started a process that transformed the illiterate and anarchic Arabs into great scholars and empire-builders and changed the course of human history. But he always thought of himself as a 'humble servant of God', and a mortal human-being. The verses quoted in this chapter and in other parts of this selection show his humanity, humility and concern for even the people who rejected him and subjected him to vicious oppression.

Say! "I have no power
Over any good or harm
To myself except as God wills.
If I had knowledge
Of the unseen, I should have
Abundance of wealth, and no misfortune
Should have touched me.
I am only a Warner,
And a Messenger of glad tidings
To those who have faith."

Qur'an, 7:188

We granted not to any man
Before you immortality:
If then you should die,
Would they live for ever?
Every soul shall have
A taste of death:
And We test you
By evil and by good
By way of trial.
To Us must you return.

Qur'an, 21:34-35

(O Muhammad)
It may be that you will consume
Yourself with grief that they
Do not become believers.

Qur'an, 26:2

(O Muhammad)
You would, perchance, torment
Yourself to death in grief
Following after them
If they believe not
In this message.

Qur'an, 18:6

We have not sent you
But as a Messenger
To all mankind,
Giving them glad tidings
And warning them against sin.
But most men know not.

Qur'an, 34:28

O Prophet! We have sent you
As a Witness, a Bearer of Good News
And a Warner,
Calling unto God by His command,
And a Luminous Source of Guidance.

Qur'an, 33:45-46

Muhammad is only a Messenger;
Many were the Messengers
Who have all passed away before him.
If he died or were slain
Will you then turn back on your heels?

Qur'an, 3:144

We sent you not, but
To be a mercy to all the worlds.

Qur'an, 21:107

MANKIND

O mankind! We created you
Male and female
And made you nations and tribes
That you may
Distinguish yourselves (in good deeds).
Surely the most honored of you
In the sight of God
Is the most virtuous of you.

Qur'an, 49:13

He (God) is the One
Who created everything
In the best form, and
He began the creation of man
From earth.
And made his progeny
From the essence
Of a humble fluid.
Then He fashioned him
In due proportion, and
Breathed into him
Of His Own Spirit.

Qur'an, 32:7-9

(The First Revelation received by Prophet Muhammad[s] in Ramadan, 610 AD)

Proclaim in the name of your
Lord and Cherisher Who Created.
Created man out of
A leech-like clot.
Proclaim and your Lord
Is Most Generous.
He Who taught with
The use of the Pen,-
Taught man what he knew not.

Qur'an, 96:1-5

And We have honored
The Human-beings; provided them
With transport on land and sea;
Given them for sustenance things
Good and pure; and conferred
On them special favors
Above a great part of Our creation.

Qur'an, 17:70

And He has raised you
From the earth
And set you up on it.

Qur'an, 11:61

Among His Signs is this,
That He created you from earth,
And then behold, you are
Mankind scattered far and wide.
And among His Signs is the fact
That He created for you mates
From among yourselves, that
You may dwell in tranquility with them,
And He has put love and affection
Between you. Surely in that are
Signs for those who reflect.
And among His Signs
Is the creation of the heavens
And the earth, and the variations
In your languages
And your colors: Surely,
In that are Signs
For those who have knowledge.

30:20-22

RELIGIOUS FREEDOM AND TOLERANCE

Considering the widespread misconceptions, among Muslims and non-Muslims alike, regarding Islam's teachings about freedom of religion and tolerance of other faiths, the verses dealing with these two subjects have been given special attention. These revolutionary ideas, promoting religious freedom, inter-faith understanding and peaceful co-existence, presented to mankind fourteen centuries ago, are clear and unambiguous and should provide some understanding of the teachings of the Qur'an.

To the Muslims who have been misled into the dark alleys of bigotry, intolerance and violence, it should be pointed out that the authority of such clear, definitive and explicit verses of the Qur'an is supreme and irrevocable and these teachings have precedence over all other sources of Islamic beliefs and practices. Any actions that contravene the spirit of these commands are tantamount to rebellion against God.

In the Qur'an, even the Prophet[s] himself is reminded again and again that he has no police powers to impose the religion on anybody and that his responsibility is only to convey clearly the Divine message. The Qur'an stresses, repeatedly, on the one hand, that only God can change people's hearts and guide them to the straight path, and on the other, that the powers of judgment, retribution and reward for actions related to one's faith and religious practices are reserved for God alone, and the state and the society are not permitted to exercise any powers in the religious sphere of life.

The following verses span the entire period of the revelation of the Qur'an, from the early phase of the mission of the Prophet[s] to the last year of his life. These quotations leave no doubt that, according to the Divine injunctions in the Qur'an, use of force and coercion, by the state or the society, in matters of faith and practice of religion, is against very clearly stated fundamental teachings of Islam and completely forbidden. The themes of religious freedom, interfaith tolerance and peaceful coexistence resonate throughout the Qur'an.

This concept of freedom of individuals to follow their own religious beliefs and practices is applicable not only to the non-Muslims (as has been suggested by some religious leaders), but also to the Muslims of various sects, beliefs and levels of adherence to the prevalent religious practices. The principle of tolerance and freedom of religion is stated in the Qur'an in universal and very comprehensive terms, applicable equally to the Muslims and non-Muslims. The verses quoted in the following pages make it evident that any acts of intolerance and violence against any non-Muslim or Muslim holding different views or beliefs and following different religious practices are diametrically opposed to the teachings of Islam.

Let there be no coercion (or compulsion)
In religion:
Truth stands out Clear from Error.
Whoever rejects the Evil
And believes in God
Has grasped the most
Trustworthy Support
That never breaks
And God hears and knows all things.

Qur'an, 2:256

Therefore, you do the reminding,
For you are only to remind,
You (O Muhammad) have no
Authority to police their affairs.

For to Us will be their return
Then it will be for Us
To call them to account.

Qur'an, 88:21-26

We know best what they say;
You (O Muhammad) have no authority
To compel them by force.
So Remind With the Qur'an
The persons
Who heed My Warning.

> Qur'an, 50:45

If it had been your Lord's Will,
They would all have believed,-
All who are on earth!
Would you then compel mankind,
Against their will, to believe?

> Qur'an, 10:99

If it had been God's Will
They would not have taken false gods.
We have made you, (O Muhammad)
Neither a controller
Nor a guardian over them.

> Qur'an, 6:107

If they then turn away,
We have not sent you
As a guardian over them.
Your duty is only to
Convey the Message.

> Qur'an, 42:48

Surely, We have revealed
The book to you in truth
For guidance of mankind.
He, then, that accepts guidance
Benefits his own self.
And he that goes astray
Injures his own soul.
And your role is not to be
A custodian over them.

> Qur'an, 39:41

Whoever does good deeds
Benefits his own soul.
Whoever works evil
It is against his own soul.
Your Lord is never
Unjust to His servants.

> Qur'an, 41:46

Say: "O you who reject faith!
I worship not that which you worship
Nor do you worship the One Who I worship.
And I will not serve that which you serve
Nor will you serve the One Who I serve.
You follow your religion
And I follow mine."

Qur'an, 109:1-6

It is not for you (O Prophet)
To guide them to the right path
But God guides
To the right path
Whom He pleases.
Whatever of good you bring forward
Benefits only your own souls,
And you shall only do so
Seeking the Presence of God.
Whatever good you spend,
Shall be rendered back to you,
And you shall not
Be treated unjustly.

Qur'an, 2:272

Invite to the Way of the Lord
With wisdom and gentle preaching,
And argue with them
In ways that are the best
And most gracious.
Your Lord knows best
Who stray from His Path,
And who accept guidance.

> Qur'an, 16:125

And if any accept guidance,
They do it for the good
Of their own souls,
And if any go astray, say:
"I am only a Warner."

> Qur'an, 27:92

We showed him the Way:
(Man has a choice)
Whether he be grateful
Or disbeliever.

> Qur'an, 76:3

Say: The Truth is
From your Lord.
Let him who will,
Believe, and let him
Who will, reject it.

Qur'an, 18:29

Whoever accepts guidance,
Receives it for his own benefit:
Whoever goes astray
Does so to his own loss.
No bearer carries
The burden of another.

Qur'an, 17:15

Say: Everyone acts
According to his own disposition:
But your Lord knows best
Who it is that is
Guided on the right path.

Qur'an, 17:84

Nay, this surely is only a reminder,
Let any who seeks guidance,
Pay attention to it.

Qur'an, 74:54-55

Surely, this is a Reminder,
Therefore, let him who desires,
Take a straight path
To his Lord.

Qur'an, 73:19 and 76:29

Say to the people who do not believe:
"You work according to your position:
We shall work according to ours."

Qur'an, 11:121

Everyone has a direction
To which he turns (in worship)
So come forward
Competing in the good deeds.

Qur'an, 2:148

Instruct those who believe
To be forgiving of those
Who (persecute them and) do not believe
In the Days of the Lord.
It is for Him to reward each
According to what they have earned.
Anyone who does a virtuous deed,
It is only to his benefit;
If one does evil,
It works only against his soul.
In the end, you will all
Return to your Lord.

Qur'an, 45:14-15

O you who believe:
(You are responsible only to)
Guard your own souls:
If you follow the guidance,
No harm will be done to you
For actions of those who stray.
The return of you all
Is to God. It is He
Who will (decide and) inform you
Of all that you do.

Qur'an, 5:105

Do not disparage those
To whom they pray besides God,
Lest they out of spite
Disparage God in their ignorance.
Thus have We made
Alluring to each people
Their own doings.
In the end, they will all
Return to their Lord.
And He shall then
Tell them the truth
Of all that they had done.

Qur'an, 6:108

And those who take
As protectors others beside Him.
God watches over them.
And you (O Prophet) are not
Responsible for their affairs.

Qur'an, 42:6

Surely this is no less than
A message to the worlds.
For him among you
Who wants to
Follow a straight path.

Qur'an, 81:27-28

And when they (the righteous) hear vain talk,
They turn away from it
And say: "To us our deeds,
And to you yours,
Peace be to you:
We seek not the ignorant."

Qur'an, 28:55

To God belong the East
And the West:
Whichever direction you turn
(In worship),
There is God's Presence.
God is All-Embracing,
All-Knowing.

Qur'an, 2:115

And they say:
"None shall enter Paradise
Except the Jews or the Christians."
Those are their vain desires.

....

Not so; whoever submits
Wholeheartedly to God
And is good to others
Will be rewarded by the Lord.
On such shall be no fear
Nor shall they grieve.

> Qur'an, 2:111-112

(O Prophet)
It is not for you (but for God)
To decide whether
He turn in mercy to them
Or punish them.
For they are indeed
The wrong-doers.

> Qur'an, 3:128

But if any reject faith,
Let not their rejection
Make you sad:
To Us is their return
And We shall tell them
The truth of their deeds:
For God knows well
All that is in men's hearts.

> Qur'an, 31:23

Obey God and obey the Messenger
And beware of evil.
If you turn back
(And disobey)
Know that Our Messenger's duty
Is only to proclaim the
Message in a clear manner.

> Qur'an, 5:92

Say: "It is God alone I worship
With my sincere devotion.
You worship what you will."

> Qur'an, 39:14-15

And (O Muhammad)
Lower your wing of kindness
To the believers who follow you.
Then if they disobey you, say:
"I am not accountable
For what you do."

Qur'an, 26:215-216

He who obeys the Messenger
Obeys God.
But if any turn away,
We have not sent you (O Muhammad)
To be a controller over them.

Qur'an, 4:80

If you did good,
It was to your own benefit,
If you did evil,
You did it against yourselves.

Qur'an, 17:7

JEWS AND CHRISTIANS
(THE PEOPLE OF THE BOOK)

In terms of the concepts of religious freedom and tolerance, the following quotations should be considered a continuation of the previous section as they add substantially to the same theme. These verses have been quoted under a separate heading because of Islam's special relationship with Judaism and Christianity, it being essentially a part of the same Abrahamic tradition of monotheism. Abraham[s], his sons Ismail[s] and Isaac[s], and all the prophets of Judaism are honored and respected and also recognized as prophets of Islam. In the Qur'an, Moses[s] and Jesus[s] are both mentioned as very prominent Messengers of God and accorded a very eminent position of honor and dignity. Similarly, the Torah, the Psalms, and the Gospel, are all recognized as works based on divine inspiration, 'containing guidance and wisdom.'

The quoted verses of the Qur'an are unambiguous. They express clearly a very strong command for the Muslims to live in peace and harmony with other religious communities. The Qur'an permits socializing with Jews and Christians, accepting their invitations and visiting their homes for dinners and inviting them to Muslim homes for sharing food with them.

The verses speak for themselves and make this concept very obvious. But to further augment this point, it would be appropriate to relate here a well-documented event from the life of Prophet Muhammad[s]:

In year 10 AH/631 AD, the last year of the life of the Prophet[s], after Najran (North Yemen) had became a part of the emerging Islamic state, a delegation of Christian clergy and missionaries from the area came to Medina to meet the Prophet[s] and have discussions about their religious beliefs and negotiations about their political relationship with their new rulers. These new subjects of the state, belonging to a different faith, were not only welcomed with honor and respect, housed in the Mosque of the Prophet[s] and allowed to worship in it according to their own religious practices, but also encouraged to engage in an open and courteous dialog about their beliefs and differences with the Islamic doctrines.

It should be pointed out here that the stay of the Christian guests in the Mosque of the Prophet[s] was not for lack of other more suitable and secular accommodations -- numerous such facilities were maintained by the Arab tribes of Medina -- but to offer them a warm personal hospitality from the Prophet[s] himself, whose own quarters were next to the mosque, and to demonstrate to his Companions his strong commitment to interfaith dialog, tolerance and harmony, and his dedication to developing an atmosphere of peaceful and amicable coexistence with people of other faiths.

When no agreement could be reached between the Prophet[s] and the visiting Christian embassy in the religious sphere, the delegation departed with due honor. They were given explicit guaranties of the safety and protection of the Christian and Jewish communities and their religious and social institutions. These promises of the Prophet[s] were honored by his Companions very meticulously and the earlier caliphs ordered the governors of Yemen not even to encourage the conversion of Christians and Jews to Islam.

It was We who revealed
The Torah: in which there
Is guidance and light.
....
And in their footsteps
We sent Jesus, the son of Mary,
Confirming the
Torah that had come before him.
We gave him the Gospel,
In that there is guidance and light.
....
Let the people of the Gospel
Judge by what God has revealed
In it. If any fail
To judge by
What God has revealed,
They are those who rebel.
To you We sent the Book
With the truth, confirming
The Scriptures that came
Before it.
....

(Continued on the next page)

(Continued from the previous page)

To all among you
Have We prescribed a Law
And a Clear Way.
If God had so willed,
He would have made you all
A single religious group, but
(His plan is) to test you
In what He has given you:
So compete with each other in
All virtuous deeds.
The goal of you all is to God.
It is He that will show you
The truth of the matter
In which you disagree.

Qur'an, 5:44-48

Those who believe (in the Qur'an),
Those who follow the
Jewish religion,
And the Sabians
And the Christians,
Any who believe in God,
And the Day of Judgment,
And perform virtuous deeds,
On them shall be no fear,
Nor shall they grieve.

Qur'an, 5:69

Surely, those who believe (in the Qur'an),
And those who follow the Jewish faith,
And the Christians and the Sabians,
Any who believe in God,
And the Last Day,
And do virtuous deeds,
They all shall have their
Reward with their Lord.
On them shall be no fear,
Nor shall they grieve.

Qur'an, 2:62

Say: We believe in God,
And the revelation given to us,
And to Abraham, Ismail,
Isaac, Jacob, and the Tribes,
And that given to Moses and Jesus,
And that given to all Prophets
From their Lord,
We make no difference
Between one and another of them:
And to Him we surrender.

Qur'an, 2:136

And argue you not
With the People of the Book
Except in the best manner
Unless it be those of them
Who have wronged you. But say,
"We believe in the revelation which has
Come down to us and in that
Which came down to you.
Our God
And your God is One;
And it is to Him
That we submit."

Qur'an, 29:46

Say: "O people of the Book!
Come to an agreement
Between us and you:
That we worship
None but God.
That we associate
No partners with Him;
That we raise not
From among ourselves,
Lords and patrons
Other than God."
If they then turn away,
Say you, "Bear witness
That we have
Submitted to God."

Qur'an, 3:64

Among the people of Moses
There is a community
Who guide and do justice
In the light of truth.

Qur'an, 7:159

Not all of them are alike:
Of the People of the Book
Are some that are upright.
They contemplate the Signs of God
During the night and
Prostrate themselves in
Worship to God.
They believe in God
And the Last Day;
They enjoin what is right
And forbid what is wrong
And they come forward
In all good works. They are
In the ranks of the Virtuous.
They will never be denied
The rewards of their good deeds;
For God knows well
Those that do right.

Qur'an, 3:113-5

So if they argue with you, say:
"I have surrendered
My whole self to God
And so have those
Who follow me."
And say to the People of the Book
And those without a Book
(People of other religions):
"Do you submit yourselves?"
If they do, they are on the right path,
But if they turn back,
Your duty is only to convey the Message;
And in God's sight
Are all His servants.

Qur'an, 3:20

JESUS[s]

Then, We sent,
Following in their footsteps
Others of our Messengers:
We sent after them
Jesus the son of Mary,
And bestowed on him the Gospel:
And We ordained in the hearts of those
Who followed him compassion and mercy.
But We did not prescribe for them
The monasticism that
They invented for themselves.
We commanded only the
Seeking for the pleasure of God,
But they did not follow it
As they should have done.
Yet We bestow on those
Among them who have faith
Their due reward, but
Many of them are
Disobedient to God.

Qur'an, 57:27

And behold! God will say:
"O Jesus, son of Mary!
Did you say unto the people,
'Take me and my mother
For two gods beside Allah?"
He will say: Glory to You!
Never could I say
What I had no right to say."

....

"Never said I to them
Except what You commanded
Me to say, that "Worship God,
My Lord and your Lord."
And I was a witness over them
While I lived among them.
When You caused my life to end,
You were the Watcher
Over them, and You are
Witness to all things.
If You punish them,
They are your servants.

(Continued on the next page)

(Continued from the previous page)

If you forgive them,
You are the Exalted in Power,
The Wise."
God will say, "This is
The Day on which
The truthful will profit
From their truth;
Theirs Are Gardens,
With rivers flowing beneath,
-Their eternal home:
God well pleased with them,
And they with God.
This is a great Achievement."

Qur'an, 5:116-119

O People of the Book!
Do not be fanatics
In your religion;[1]
Nor say anything
About God but the truth.
Christ Jesus, the son of Mary
Was a Messenger of God,
And His Word,
Which He bestowed on Mary,
And a Spirit (of Mercy) from Him:
So believe in God and His Messengers.
Say not 'Three': Desist.
It will be better for you.
For God is only One God:
Glory be to Him. Far Exalted is He
Above having a son.
To Him belong all things
In the heavens and earth.
And enough is God
As a Guardian for all.

Qur'an, 4:171

---

1. This injunction against fanaticism and over-zealous attitude, addressed here to the People of the Book, is not in any way limited to them, it is also a very important command for the Muslims.

SOCIAL INTERACTION WITH NON-MUSLIMS

The following quotations from the Qur'an visualize a society in which people of different faiths not only live peacefully and harmoniously alongside each other, but also feel integrated in a tolerant atmosphere. According to the quoted verse of the Qur'an, Muslims are allowed to have courteous and friendly social relationships with followers of all other religions as long as they are not hostile to Islam or repressive and unjust to the Muslims.

With Jews and Christians, the scope of relationship goes much further. As they are considered followers of the same monotheistic Abrahamic tradition, Muslims are not only permitted to develop friendly social ties with them, but also allowed to invite Jews and Christians to their homes for sharing food, and accept invitations to Jewish and Christian homes for the same purpose.

Interfaith marriages between Muslim men and Jewish and Christian women are fully sanctioned. It is impossible to envision a marriage between adherents of two different faiths without mutual tolerance and respect for each other's faith and religious traditions. Such marriages also presuppose a society in which different religious groups are living side-by-side in a peaceful atmosphere, and interacting with each other in social and cultural activities.

This day, all things good and pure
Are made lawful for you.
The food of the People of the Book
Is lawful for you.
And yours is lawful for them.
Lawful for you (in marriage) are
(not only)
The virtuous women who are believers,
But also virtuous women
Among the People of the Book.
....
When you give them their marital gifts
And live with them in honor,
Not lewdness, nor taking them as lovers.

Qur'an, 5:5[p

God does not forbid you
To have friendly and equitable
Relationship with those
(Non-Muslims) who
Do not fight you on account of religion
Nor expel you from your homes.
God loves those who are just.

Qur'an, 60:8

ALL DEEDS HAVE CONSEQUENCES

Whoever submit themselves
To God, and do virtuous deeds,
They will have their reward
With their Lord.
On them shall be no fear,
Nor shall they grieve.

Qur'an, 2:112

Whoever performs virtuous deeds,
Man or woman, and has faith,
Surely to them will We give
A life that is good and pure,
And We will bestow on such
Their reward
According to the best
Of their actions.

Qur'an, 16:97

Whoever works any acts
Of righteousness and has faith
His endeavors will not be rejected:
We shall record it in his favor.

Qur'an, 21:94

On no soul does God place
A burden greater than it can bear.
It gets every good that it earns
And it suffers every ill that it earns.

> Qur'an, 2:286

If any do virtuous deeds
--Be they male or female –
And have faith,
They will enter Paradise,
And not the least injustice
Will be done to them.

> Qur'an, 4:124

Then anyone who has done
An atom's weight of good
Shall see it!
And anyone who has done
An atom's weight of evil
Shall see it.

> Qur'an, 99:7-8

Every soul is captive
Of its own deeds.

> Qur'an, 74:38

ONLY DEFENSIVE WAR PERMITTED

To those who are attacked,
Permission is granted
To fight back
Because they have been oppressed;
And certainly, God is Most Powerful
For their aid;-
They are those who have
Been expelled from their homes unjustly
Except that they say, "God is our Lord."
If God did not check one group of people
By means of another,
There would surely have been
Destroyed Monasteries, Churches,
Synagogues, and Mosques, in which all
God's name is commemorated abundantly.

Qur'an, 22:39-40

Fight in the cause of God
Against those who fight you,
But do not commit aggression.
God loves not the aggressors.

Qur'an, 2:190

If enemy inclines towards peace
You also incline towards peace
And put your trust in God.

Qur'an, 8:61

And fight them on until
There is no more persecution,
And Judgment about religion
Belongs to God completely.
But if they stop (persecution),
Then surely
God sees all that they do.

Qur'an, 8:39

And fight them on until
There is no more persecution,
And religion becomes a matter
For only God to judge.
But if they stop (persecution and fighting)
Let there be no hostility
Except to those
Who practice oppression.

Qur'an, 2:193

PIETY

It is not Piety
That you turn your faces (in worship)
Towards East or West.
But Piety is to believe in God
And the Life Hereafter
And the Angels and the Book
And the Prophets;
To spend of your wealth
Out of love for God
For your relatives,
For orphans,
For the destitute,
For the homeless,
For those who ask,
And for those burdened with servitude,
To be steadfast in prayer and to give charity,
To fulfill the promises and contracts made,
And to be firm and patient
In pain and suffering
And difficult circumstances
And in periods of panic.
Such are the people of Piety.

Qur'an, 2:177

CHARITY

The parable of those who spend
Their wealth in the way of God
Is that of a grain;
It sprouts seven ears,
And each ear has a hundred grains.
God gives manifold increase to whom
He pleases, and God cares
For all and He knows all things.
Those who spend their wealth
In the cause of God,
And follow not up what they have given
With mention of their generosity
Or with insult or harm, - For them,
Their reward is with their Lord:
On them shall be no fear,
Nor shall they grieve.
Kind words
And covering of (others') faults
Are better than charity
(That is) followed by hurt.
God is Free of all wants
And He is most Forbearing.

Qur'an, 2:261-63

And they have been commanded
No more than this:
To worship God
Offering their sincere devotion,
Being true in faith,
To establish regular prayer
And to give charity, and that is
The religion right and straight.

Qur'an, 98:5

And give to your relatives
A share (from your wealth), and
Also to those in need,
And to the homeless,
But squander not your wealth
In the manner of a spendthrift.

Qur'an, 17:26

If you have to turn (the needy persons) away,
Because you (lack the means and)
Are awaiting God's bounty,
Say to them gentle words of kindness.

Qur'an, 17:28

JUSTICE AND FAIR DEALING

O You who believe!
Stand out firmly for God as
Champions of justice and fairness.
And let not hatred of
Any nation
Incite you to
Deviate from justice.
Always be just and equitable,
That is closest to Piety:
And revere God.
For God is fully aware
Of all that you do.

Qur'an, 5:8

O Believers
Stand out firmly as champions of justice,
And witnesses to God
Even against yourselves,
Or your parents, or your relatives,
And whether it be against
Rich or poor
For God can best protect both.
Follow not your desires
To swerve from justice,
And if you distort facts
Or decline to do justice, surely
God is fully aware
Of all that you do.

Qur'an, 4:135

Say: My Lord has commanded justice,
And that you set your whole selves to Him,
At every time and place of worship,
And call upon Him
Making your devotion sincere.
Such as He created you in the beginning,
So shall you return."

Qur'an, 7:29

God commands you
To deliver all Trusts
To those to whom they are due;
And when you judge
Between people
That you judge with justice;

Qur'an, 4:58

O you who believe
Fulfill your contracts.

Let not hatred of a group
That barred you from the Holy Mosque[1]
Incite you to commit acts
Of injustice against them.
Cooperate with each other
In acts of righteousness and virtue.
And do not help each other
In sin and aggression.

Qur'an, 5:1-2

---

1. The Unbelievers at Mecca had denied the Muslims access to the Ka'ba and barred them from performing Hajj (pilgrimage). This verse forbids the Muslims from being vengeful and from taking any unjust action against their enemies.

God commands justice,
The doing of good,
And giving to kith and kin,
And He forbids all indecent acts,
And evil and rebellion.

> Qur'an, 16:90

"And O people! Give
Just measure and weight,
Nor withhold from the people
The things that are their due:
Commit no evil in the land
With intent to do mischief.

> Qur'an, 11:85

Give full measure when you measure
And weigh with an accurate balance:
That is better and fairer
In the final determination.

> Qur'an, 17:35

Whenever you speak, speak justly,
Even if a near relative is concerned;-
And fulfill the Covenant of God.

> Qur'an, 6:152

PARENTS

Your Lord has decreed
That you worship none but Him,
And that you be kind
To your parents.
Whether one or both of them
Attain old age in your life,
Say not to them a word
Of contempt, nor repel them.
But address them
In terms of honor.

And with kindness
Lower to them the wing
Of humility, and say,
"My Lord, bestow on them
Your Mercy even as they
Cherished me in childhood."

Qur'an, 17:23-24

MISCELLANEOUS

Nor come near to adultery:
For it is an abomination
And an evil path.

Qur'an, 17:32

Nor take life
- God has made it sacred -
except
In the pursuit of justice.

Qur'an, 17:33

O you who believe!
Intoxicants and Gambling,
Sacrificing to stones and idols
And Divination by arrows (etc.)
All are abominations –
Handiwork of the devil.
Keep away from such things
So that you may prosper.

(Qur'an, 5:90)

O you who believe!
Let not some people among you
Mock and ridicule others.

....

Nor defame, nor be
Sarcastic to each other
Nor insult each other by
Offensive nick-names.

....

Avoid suspicion as much as possible
For suspicion in some cases is a sin.
And spy not on each other
Nor speak ill of each other
Behind their backs.

Qur'an, 49:11-12

And Good and Evil cannot
Be equal.
Respond to other's evil deed
With what is good
(And as a result)
One who was your enemy
May become your loyal friend and confidant.

Qur'an, 41:34

And covet not
Those things in which
God has bestowed His gifts
More freely on some of you
Than on others:
To men
Belongs what they earn
And to women what they earn.
And pray to God for His bounty,
For God has full knowledge
Of all things.

Qur'an, 4:32

Come not near to the
Orphan's property
Except to improve it,
Until he attain the age
Of full strength;
And fulfill your contracts, for
You shall be held accountable for them.

Qur'an, 17:34

And every nation has its term,
(Of rise and fall):
When that term
Is reached, not an hour
Can they cause delay,
Nor an hour can they advance it.

> Qur'an, 7:34

These days (of varying fortunes)
We circulate among people.

> Qur'an, 3:140

Surely, never does God change
The conditions of a people
Until they change
What is in themselves.

> Qur'an, 13:11

No bearer carries
The burden of another.
Man can have nothing
But what he strives for.

> Qur'an, 53:38-39

There is not an animal on the earth
Nor a being that flies on its wings,
But (forms part of)
Communities like you.

Qur'an, 6:38

Every soul shall have
A taste of death.
And We test you
By evil and by good
By way of trial.
To Us will you return.

Qur'an, 21:35

And there is not a thing
But its treasures are with Us.
We only reveal
(And lead man to discover)
Parts of it
In measured quantities.

Qur'an, 15:21

And swell not your cheek
Scornfully at people,
Nor walk in insolence
Through the earth;
For God loves not
Any arrogant boaster.
And be moderate in your pace,
And lower your voice; for the harshest
Of sounds is the braying of the ass.

Qur'an, 31:18-19

And walk not on the earth
With arrogance: For you
Cannot rend the earth asunder,
Nor reach the mountains in height.

Qur'an, 17:37

And servants of God Most Gracious
Are those who
Tread the earth in humility,
And when the ignorant talk to them,
They say, "Peace!"

Qur'an, 25:63

Our Lord!
Let not our hearts deviate
After You have guided us.
But grant us Mercy
From Your Own Presence.
And You are the
Grantor of bounties
Without measure.

Qur'an, 3:8

O My Lord!
Grant me Wisdom,
And join me
With the righteous.

Qur'an, 26:83

Without doubt,
In the remembrance of God
Do hearts find comfort.

Qur'an, 13:28

English Translations of the Qur'an

Since the publication, in 1734, of <u>The Al Koran of Mohammed</u> by George Sale (1697-1736), dozens of English translations of the Qur'an have been produced, especially in the last few decades, and most of them are still in print. Only a short list of readily available translations is being included here, with brief notes about some of the translators.

Ali, Abdullah Yusuf; 1872-1953
> <u>The Holy Qur'an; Text, Translation and Commentary.</u>
> First published in 1934. Reprinted many times.

Both the original and a revised version published by the government of Saudi Arabia under the title <u>The Holy Qur-an, English translation of the Meanings and Commentary</u> are currently available. Detailed foot-notes and introductions to the chapters make it easier to understand the text.

Ali, Muhammad, Maulana, 1874-1951.
> <u>The Holy Qur'an, Arabic text with English translation and commentary</u>, Lahore, First Published 1917. Revised edition, 1951. Many reprints, for example: Dublin, Oh, 2002.

This was the first English translation of the Qur'an by a Muslim and it won high praise, both in the subcontinent and in England.

Arberry, A.J., 1905-1969.
> <u>The Koran interpreted</u>. First published in 1955, and reprinted numerous times.

A.J. Arberry was a renowned scholar of Islam and Sir Adams Professor of Arabic at the University of Cambridge, England. He wrote many works on Islam and Sufism, and his translation of the Qur'an is considered to be one of the finest in linguistic style and the best by a non-Muslim scholar.

Asad, Muhammad; 1900-1992.
>The Message of the Quran. Gibraltar, 1980.

Born Leopold Weiss in Germany as a grandson of an Orthodox Jewish Rabbi, he changed his name to Muhammad Asad when he converted to Islam in 1926. Asad dedicated his life to the study of Islamic literature and Arab society and became one of its prominent intellectuals and a well-known reformist leader. "In its intellectual engagement with the text and in the subtle and profound understanding of the pure classical Arabic of the Koran, Asad's interpretation is of a power and intelligence without rival in English." -- *The Guardian*

Khalifa, Rashad, 1935-1990.
> The Glorious Quran; an authorized English version, Tucson, AZ, 1981. Many subsequent editions.

Rashad Khalifa published his translation of the Qur'an in 1981 which was well-received at that time. He claimed to have discovered some unique numerical peculiarities ('miracles' in his words) of the text of the Qur'an. Later, when he put forward a claim to be a Messenger of God, strong opposition to his writings emerged among the Muslims. He was murdered in 1990, allegedly by a conservative Muslim group.

Pickthall, Mohammed Marmaduke; 1875-1936.
> The Meaning of the Glorious Koran was first published in 1930. The book is still in print..

Born William Pickthall to an Anglican clergyman, he started studying Islam at an early age and became a Muslim in 1917. His work was the first English translation of the Qur'an by a European Muslim. It still retains considerable popularity.